An opini

CW01508592

LONDON BOOKSHOPS

Written by
SONYA BARBER
and JAMES MANNING

Walden Books (no.25)

INFORMATION IS DEAD.
LONG LIVE OPINION.

Book-buying has never been easier! Your Amazon algorithm can suggest a book, and then a robot can deliver it this afternoon. Why bother with a guidebook to London's best bookshops?

We think nothing beats the magic of walking into a quiet shop full of printed treasure. In an age of online shopping and instantaneous gratification, it's more important than ever to enjoy real bookshops. If, like us, you cherish the experience of perusing curated shelves, getting an insightful recommendation from a bookseller and walking away with something that might just change your life – this book is for you.

Martin
Hoxton Mini Press

BookBar (no.24)
Right: South Bank Book Market (no.54)

Art Cards

John Sandoe Books (no.56)

READ YOUR WAY
THROUGH LONDON

There's no getting around it: real-life bookshops are widely presumed to be going the way of pie and mash and VHS. But after visiting more than 80 of them, we're happy to report that London's bookselling scene is alive and thriving. Not only are many stalwarts (like Hatchards, no.7, founded in 1797) still drawing crowds, but new bookshops are springing up all the time, bringing fresh perspectives to an old trade. Several, like Common Press (no.41), have only opened their doors in the last few years.

Even if buying online has gotten easier (and sometimes cheaper), there's no mystery as to why people still love buying books in person: nothing beats the atmosphere of a bookshop. Whether it's a chaotic shuffle of second-hand reads (see Hurlingham Books, no.55), or a super-stylish selection like those you'll find at Donlon Books (no.34) or Libreria (no.33), browsing in person feels like stepping into a world of boundless possibilities.

Bookshops – and the recommendations of knowledgeable booksellers – bring much-missed serendipity to our algorithm-driven lives. When you set foot inside a bookshop, there's every chance you'll come away with something that changes the way you see the world.

While the 200,000 books at Waterstones Piccadilly (no.5) offer vast choice, a specialist bookshop is a sanctuary. For recipes, there's Books for Cooks (no.57); for art, Koenig Books (no.37); for radical politics, Housmans (no.23). All are staffed by people who know and love the books they sell. By shopping at an independent bookshop, you're supporting their passion – and future generations of readers.

Often, bookshops are meeting points for a whole community – whether that be LGBTQIA+ Londoners at Gay's The Word (no.12), anarchists at Freedom Press (no.38) or witches at Treadwell's (no.18). Many have fought tough battles to stay open, threatened by Amazon, rent hikes, relocations and even firebombs; the diversity of London's bookshops is only matched by their tenacity.

As a couple of London-born book lovers, we each have our own tastes: James can spend hours leafing through maps and modernist novels; Sonya has an impressive library of art, food and photography books. Together, our collections threaten to take over our flat – and now we have a toddler, our days are spent tripping over wild things and cats in hats. The hardest part of compiling this list has been deciding what to leave out... that, and not overloading our shelves with even more enticing things to read.

Sonya Barber and James Manning
London, 2024

BEST FOR...

When you don't know what you're looking for

For help navigating the latest publications, the team at the London Review Bookshop (no.13) are second to none. Pages of Hackney (no.43) gives each bookseller a whole shelf to showcase their faves, and the thoughtful staff picks at Gay's The Word (no.12) are a brilliant primer to the many facets of LGBTQIA+ identities.

Getting kids reading

Pickled Pepper (no.31) and The Alligator's Mouth (no.63) are devoted entirely to children and young adults, with loads of great events, too. Nomad Books (no.62) and Owl Bookshop (no.21) both give a lot of space to little ones and Round Table Books (no.53), which started out as kids-only, is the best place in town for inclusive children's literature.

An exclusive experience

Book an appointment to browse the shelves of fashionably eclectic 'visual reference' books at IDEA (no.3), or the feminist first editions at The Second Shelf (no.20) – you'll get plenty of help, and maybe even a cup of tea.

Beautiful illustration

Gosh! (no.9) has the most comprehensive range of comics, graphic novels and all things illustrated. Artwords (no.40) and Magma (no.15) are both excellent for illustration as well as the other visual arts – both have great kids' sections, too.

Bagging a bargain

Skoob Books (no.16) is one of the best places to bargain-hunt, with Judd Books (no.11) around the corner also stocking a great number of remaindered titles at knockdown prices. Bookmongers (no.52) specialises in remainders, with many recent bestsellers available at up to half-price.

Bringing literature to life

Morocco Bound (no.45) has evening events almost daily, offering up quizzes, open mics and craft beer. Burley Fisher's (no.35) annual literary festival goes even further. Libreria (no.33) host author events in the shop and across the road at the tangerine-hued Second Home workspace.

Stopping for a snack

Rest your weary legs in the soothing cafe at Common Press (no.41). Stop for lunch at Books for Cooks (no.57), where recipes come straight from the bookshop shelves. For something stronger, BookBar (no.24) turns from a cafe to a bar (with books, of course) as the evening approaches.

Something a bit different

It doesn't come more quirky than Word on the Water (no.26), London's only floating bookshop, while the Garden Museum (no.51) has the city's only bookshop in a deconsecrated church. For something more profane, check out Treadwell's (no.18) or Watkins Books in Cecil Court (no.14). And the prize for most unusual books goes to Donlon (no.34).

1

DAUNT BOOKS

Cosmopolitan Marylebone stunner

Daunt now has branches across London and beyond, but its Marylebone flagship remains the most striking. Its cathedral-like central atrium is an Edwardian marvel: lofty galleries set on two stories are overlooked by clear skylights, and the oak shelves are organised not by author or topic, but country. The ground floor is Europe, with Prague guidebooks sitting next to Kafka and Kundera, and Orwell's *Homage to Catalonia* flanked by Basque language courses. The basement stretches from North America (Frederick Douglass, Michelle Obama, Bill Bryson) to the Middle East (*One Thousand and One Nights*, Khalil Gibran, the Iraq War). It's a truly breathtaking space and concept. No wonder Daunt totes are the quintessential accessory for London bookworms.

83–84 Marylebone High Street, w1u 4QW
Nearest station: Baker Street
Other locations: Holland Park, Cheapside,
Hampstead, Belsize Park
dauntbooks.co.uk

2

THE PHOTOGRAPHERS'
GALLERY BOOKSHOP

Frame-worthy publications

The London home for all things photography lies sandwiched between the madness of Oxford Street and Soho. As you'd imagine, the basement bookshop has the city's most extensive assortment of photography titles. All the big names are here – Nan Goldin, William Eggleston, Lee Miller, Martin Parr – plus loads of exciting cutting-edge snappers you may not have heard of. It's not just hi-spec coffee-table monographs, either – there are also small-press fanzines, fun gifty bits and a thoughtful edit of everything that informs the whole photographic process, from history and politics to technique and theory. If a visit inspires you to upgrade from shooting on your iPhone, they also conveniently sell film and cameras.

16–18 Ramillies Street, W1F 7LW
Nearest station: Oxford Circus
bookshop.thephotographersgallery.org.uk

3

IDEA

The coolest bookshop in London?

Scarecrows! Snoopy! Sensual swimwear! You won't find such a fantastically panoramic mix of vintage books anywhere else in London. For over a decade, well-connected writer David Owen and photographer Angela Hill have sourced rare 'visual reference' works on art, fashion, music, interiors, textiles, architecture and film, as well as publishing their own cool-as-anything photography books. Today, they have a concession in Dover Street Market (which also sells their cult line of caps and totes) and a secret room of 'superbooks' in Soho where they'll show you their goodies by appointment. Make a beeline for the signed section which features everyone from Basquiat and Hockney to Seinfeld and Jane Fonda.

101 Wardour Street, W1F 0UG
Nearest station: Piccadilly Circus
ideanow.online

4

MAGCULTURE

London's paen to the glossies

We'll admit that magazines aren't *exactly* the same as books… but magCulture is such an enthusiastic celebration of print that it wouldn't be right to skip it on a technicality. This modernist white, red and black space in a former newsagent in Clerkenwell houses an overwhelmingly comprehensive array of mags covering every topic imaginable: politics to printmaking, fashion to football, working life, climbing and travel to whisky, coffee and tea. Parked by the door you'll find a rack of new arrivals curated afresh every week alongside impeccable staff picks. (For more, check out magCulture's blog – which ran for ten years before the shop opened – and its podcast interviews with magazine makers.) The sign outside says 'We love magazines' and after a session here, you'll feel just the same.

270 St John Street, EC1V 4PE
Nearest station: Angel
magculture.com

5

WATERSTONES PICCADILLY

A behemoth flagship

Stretching across six floors of a superb modernist structure that formerly housed the Simpsons department store, this is the largest bookshop not just in London, but the whole of Europe. With a stonking eight miles of shelves, there's room for pretty much everything here: 200,000 books, apparently. The second floor gets a special mention with its epic kids' section and dizzying selection of manga. There are three cafes (including a panoramic fifth-floor bar with excellent views over Westminster), free Wi-Fi, decent public toilets and a sneaky back entrance. Yes, it's the imposing flagship of the UK's biggest high-street book chain (so not quite your friendly local), but this is an indispensable literary amenity.

203–206 Piccadilly, W1J 9HD
Nearest station: Piccadilly Circus
waterstones.com/bookshops/piccadilly

6

JARNDYCE

Approachable antiquarians

Family-run Jarndyce – a reference to the never-ending legal case from Charles Dickens's *Bleak House* – is a heavyweight antiquarian bookseller with the catalogues to prove it. They've been trading for over 50 years but their tourist-friendly location opposite the British Museum lures in curious passers-by as well as the serious collector. The books on display are on the more affordable side, and they stock fun literary ephemera like card games and the shop's own 'bizarre books' greetings cards and calendars. There's a coal fire in winter, scores of leather spines and glimpses of an intriguing back room. A bust of Dickens – one of the shop's specialities, naturally – gazes down from the shelves. It feels like the kind of place he would have approved of.

46 Great Russell Street, WC1B 3PA
Nearest station: Tottenham Court Road
jarndyce.co.uk

7

HATCHARDS

Posh Piccadilly institution

Right next door to Fortnum & Mason, grocers to the king, Hatchards offers nourishment of a different sort – though just as upmarket. It was founded in 1797 and its genteel atmosphere – striking black shelves, pea soup-coloured carpets and royal warrants on the wall – is like stepping into a National Trust property. A pleasing (if maze-like) layout stretches out from a gently creaking central wooden staircase, taking you through four storeys of rooms and corridors devoted to different topics: kids' reference books; gardens and cooking; detective fiction; a huge history section on the ground floor, and full shelves for Shakespeare, Agatha Christie and P. G. Wodehouse. The top floor is the best, with the sparsest crowds, books on all the visual arts and an attic of antiquarian finds.

187 Piccadilly, W1J 9LE
Nearest station: Piccadilly Circus
hatchards.co.uk

8

FOYLES

A biggie but a goodie

Since opening its doors on Charing Cross Road in 1906, Foyles has been a beacon for bibliophiles. The latest incarnation of the flagship store is its most epic yet, with six floors and an events space. Fuel up on caffeine in the chilled cafe before meandering down through the floors that surround the central atrium. Each has its own distinct personality and enthusiasts – you'll find eager linguists milling about the notably brilliant foreign-language literature, Japanophiles absorbed in the graphic novels, students poring over the fashion books and parents clutching Gruffalo toys down on the kids' floor. Beyond books, there are jazz CDs and vinyl, drawers of classical sheet music, racks of world-cinema DVDs and even art supplies.

107 Charing Cross Road, WC2H 0DT
Nearest station: Tottenham Court Road
Other locations: South Bank, Waterloo, Stratford
foyles.co.uk

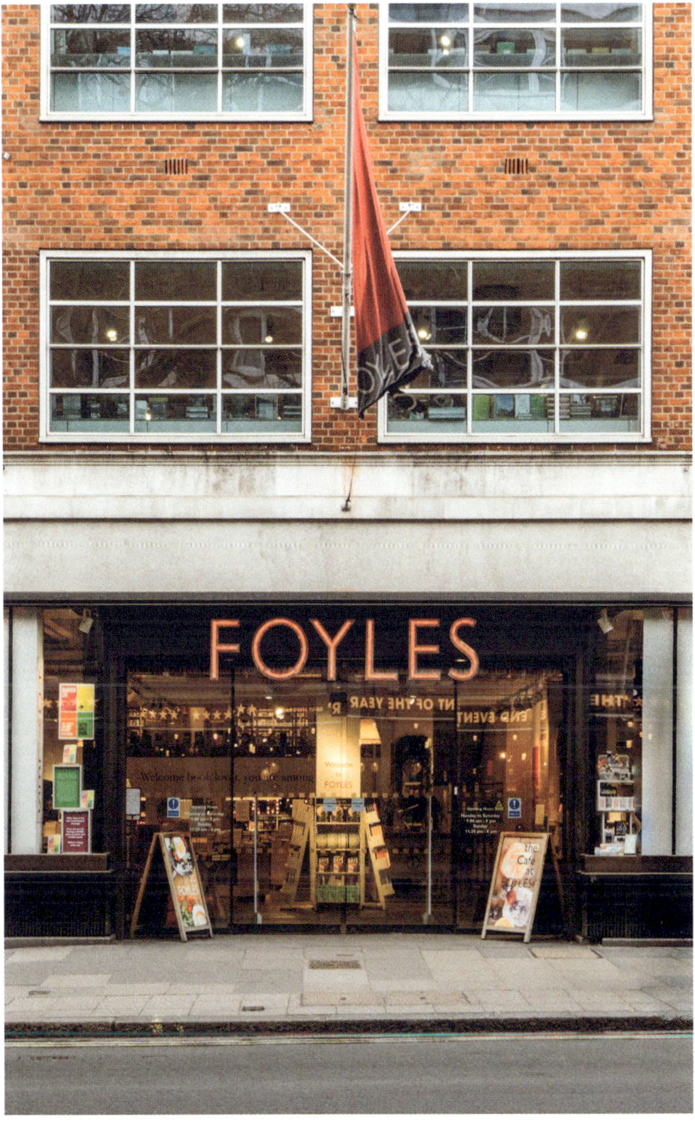
FOYLES
the Café at FOYLES

9

GOSH! COMICS

Riotous celebration of illustration

Bosh! As soon as you enter Gosh! you're hit by a riot of colour: eye-popping graphic covers proudly facing out, illustrated posters on the walls and inviting graphic book artwork celebrated on every surface. With one of the most extensive selections of comics in London, Gosh! will have familiar faces even for newcomers – say hello to the Marvel Universe, Moomins, Simpsons and Tintin, along-side an abundance of niche small-press publications to enthral the most seasoned readers. Downstairs is where the real geekery gets going, with manga mania and racks of superhero comics ready to be rifled through. If stories aren't your bag, there are also illustrated non-fiction books covering everything from the history of wine to hip-hop.

1 Berwick Street, W1F 0DR
Nearest station: Leicester Square
goshlondon.com

10

RIBA BOOKSHOP

Grand Designs in book form

The inspiring Royal Institute of British Architecture is worth a visit for the Art Deco site alone, but their bookshop brings it to a whole other level. Pros come to Portland Place for shelves stacked with reference books, regulation manuals and specialist writing across sustainable materials, designing for disability and monographs delving into the work of every architect imaginable. Enthusiasts will appreciate the impressive range of DIY and remodelling fodder, with practical books on interior and garden design, neat guides to architecture-spotting in London and a kids' section with playful books on construction. Visualise your dream home over a chai latte in the little cafe.

66 Porland Place, W1B 1AD
Nearest station: Regent's Park
ribabooks.com/riba-bookshop-london

OASE 116

The Architect
as Public Intellectual

De architect
als publieke intellectueel

Journal for Architecture
Tijdschrift voor Architectuur

OASE #115
Inter-
feren-
ces:
Mo-
ving
across
Euro-
pean
Arc

oase #114

optimi m
or
ust

optimi
o

11

JUDD BOOKS

A veritable Bloomsbury icon

Set up in the 1990s by two booksellers from Housmans (no.23), Judd is regularly packed to the gills with students from the local universities who flock here to browse the keenly priced stock and chew over their essays in the aisles. Hefty academic tomes and art books go for less than a tenner, plus there's a smattering of fiction, poetry and drama. Downstairs at the back lies a cavernous basement that goes big on the social sciences. Whether you're reading up on witchcraft or The Beatles, Abstract Impressionism or psychoanalysis, at least one of the 50,000 titles here should catch your eye. Don't miss the blue plaque opposite commemorating the ultimate literary power couple: Mary and Percy Shelley.

82 Marchmont Street, WC1N 1AG
Nearest station: Russell Square
juddbooks.com

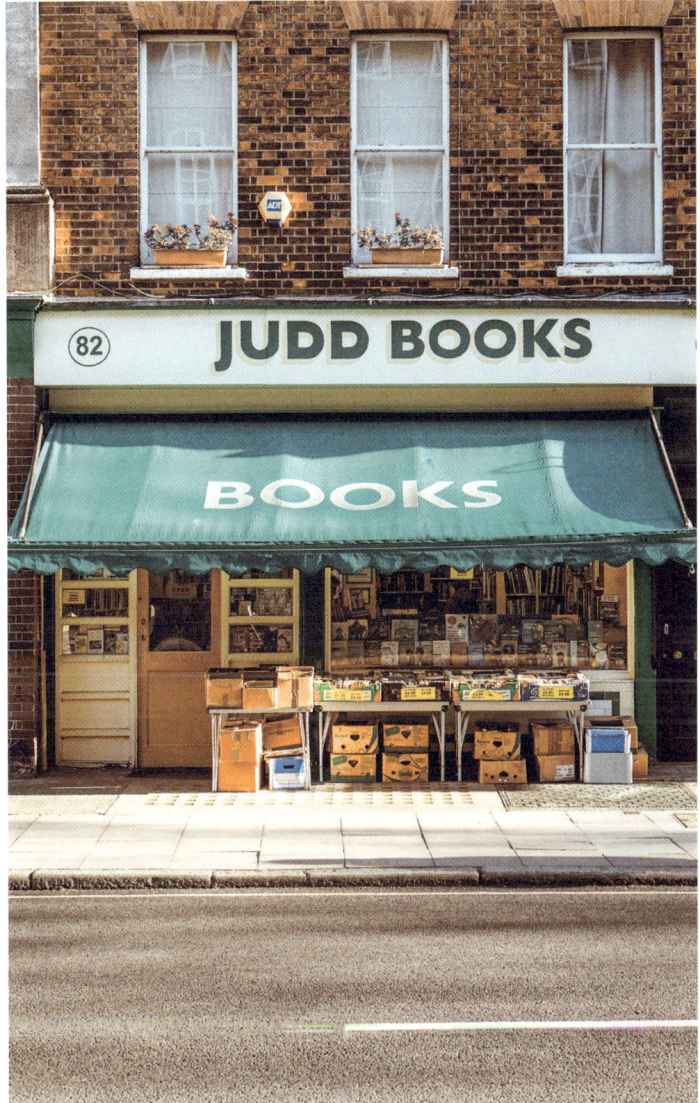

12
GAY'S THE WORD

Britain's finest LGBTQIA+ bookshop

Since opening here in 1979, Gay's The Word has been a crucial meeting point for London's queer community, successfully fighting off homophobic government raids in the 1980s and the threat of closure in the 2000s. Its welcoming vibe, community noticeboard and poignant collection of LGBTQIA+ memorabilia are testament both to its history and continuing importance. Shelves hold books for all members of the community, from gay poetry and lesbian fiction to trans memoirs, including books for kids from queer families and teens coming out. Hand-written staff recommendations just add to the warm atmosphere. Pick up an armful of books – plus a T-shirt and tote bag – and support a proper institution.

66 Marchmont St, WC1N 1AB
Nearest station: Russell Square
gaystheword.co.uk

13

LONDON REVIEW BOOKSHOP

A bastion of literary delight

The fortnightly *London Review of Books* is the UK's most esteemed literary tastemaker, and their Bloomsbury bookshop its cheerful fortress. Staff picks by the entrance feature 60 titles at a time, from experimental novelist Sheila Heti to Marxist philosopher Frantz Fanon, and a revolving door of displays highlight their 'Author of the Month' or the latest literary prize shortlists. See if you can get a poetry recommendation from John Clegg, who voices their certifiably hilarious Twitter feed, or purchase a marvellously curated box themed on satire, scent or apocalypse. Their woman-led Cake Shop cafe, with its sumptuous pastries and excellent dal, is worth its own pilgrimage.

14–16 Bury Place, WC1A 2JL
Nearest station: Holborn
londonreviewbookshop.co.uk

14

CECIL COURT

London's most bookish street

Few streets on Earth are as densely packed with literature as Cecil Court: of the 22 shops on this famous street near Leicester Square, one third are bookshops. Five centuries of rare books and maps await you at friendly antiquarians Bryars & Bryars. Browse sheet music, concert programmes and musical biographies at Travis & Emery, or brave a tarot reading at esoteric specialists Watkins Books, established in 1901 and comprehensively stocking arcane practices from astral projection to zen. Marchpane is a rabbit hole of children's classics, while Goldsboro and Tindley And Everett specialise in first editions. And if you'd prefer something slightly more contemporary, olive-fronted Tenderbooks publish and sell fresh indie art books and ephemera.

Cecil Court, WC2N 4HE
Nearest station: Leicester Square
cecilcourt.co.uk

15

MAGMA

Stylish books, games and gifts

Design aficionados Magma have been serving up the best in visual culture since the early 2000s: books on design, architecture, travel, nature and food, plus magazines and plenty for London's coolest under-18s. Everything is knowingly curated and displayed, frequently cover-out. The Covent Garden flagship is a bright, white-shelved space that goes big on gifts and stationery, stocking plenty of illustrated card decks and games, jigsaw puzzles and cute prints. The smaller, concrete-floored Clerkenwell branch is a little more bookish, but still has room for a Moomin-heavy gift range.

29 Short's Gardens, WC2H 9AP
Nearest station: Covent Garden
Other location: Clerkenwell
magma-shop.com

16

SKOOB BOOKS

A cornucopia of second-hand books

It's not all that easy to find Skoob, hidden away down an unassuming staircase round the back of the monolithic Brunswick Centre. And you might not expect much from this industrial-looking basement furnished with pipes, concrete pillars and about a mile of DIY-looking wooden bookshelves. But don't be deceived: you could spend hours down here browsing second-hand bargains: novels from Marcel Proust to Dan Brown, endless non-fiction from film to theology, pamphlets piled on a piano and a bold display of classic orange Penguin paperbacks – perfect for a spontaneously purchased park read.

66 The Brunswick, off Marchmont St, WC1N 1AE
Nearest station: Russell Square
skoob.com

17

STANFORDS

A map-lover's Shangri-La

It was a sad day for cartophiles when Stanfords closed its legendary Long Acre shop after 117 years, but they've found a new home just around the corner. It's a touch smaller, but remains a spiritual home for wanderers – and yes, there's still a very nice cafe. A-Zs, French wine guides, historic British town plans, Himalayan trekking routes, Asian railway networks, maritime charts and even globes – if you're looking for any variety of physical map, you'll find it in their vast basement. And if they don't have it, they can probably run it off for you using their massive on-site printer. Whether you're looking to spark travel inspiration, browse guidebooks or just cast off with memoirs and globetrotting fiction, this is the place to channel your inner Phileas Fogg.

7 Mercer Walk, WC2H 9FA
Nearest station: Covent Garden
stanfords.co.uk

18

TREADWELL'S BOOKS

Witchy but welcoming

Looking to lay hands on a spell book, tarot deck, Ouija board or crystal ball? Treadwell's is the place. Though a relative newcomer to London's occult scene (it was established in 2003, whereas nearby Atlantis dates to 1922), Treadwell's quickly became an institution among the city's Wiccans, pagans and spiritualists. It looks (and smells) exactly as you'd hope a witch's library would: dark wood, drapey curtains, carved masks and incense. The shelves are lined with new and second-hand volumes on all aspects of magick, from practical manuals and spiritual zines to biographies of leading magi, esoteric travel guides and occult literature. The busy calendar of workshops and lectures offers plenty of opportunities to dip your toe into the craft.

33 Store St, WC1E 7BS
Nearest station: Goodge Street
treadwells-london.com

19

CLIMAX BOOKS HQ

X-rated art books and literature

Smutty Soho feeling too sanitised these days? Slink down an alley off D'Arblay Street, buzz in at number five, climb the ladder-like staircase and step into Climax. There's some seriously highbrow filth here: rare first editions of Yayoi Kusama's self-published orgy pamphlets, John Waters on sex in art history, vintage erotica by Anaïs Nin... plus lit and crit with an eye on sex and sexuality: Germaine Greer, Kathy Acker, Jean Baudrillard, Chris Kraus. All this plus large-format photography, fashion, film and subculture titles, rare zines, catalogues, VHS tapes and postcards. And don't worry, the vibe is decidedly unseedy – more graphic design studio than peep show.

5 Wardour Mews, WIF 8AL
Nearest station: Tottenham Court Road
climaxbooks.com

20

THE SECOND SHELF

A treasured feminist collection

Writer and book expert Allison Devers founded The Second Shelf to address the gender inequality in the world of rare and antiquarian books, collecting rare books, manuscripts, signed copies and first editions by women and non-binary writers to sell in her Soho shop. The doors sadly closed in 2021, but Allison now has a private store in Gospel Oak which feels even more intimate. Glance around and you'll spot lots of authors you'll know and many you won't, as well as cool collectables like a signed Yoko Ono poem or Sylvia Plath's old tartan skirt. Book an appointment, tell her your favourite writers and she'll pull together a unique, curated selection just for you.

Unit 42, Spectrum House,
32–34 Gordon House Road, NW5 1LP
Nearest station: Gospel Oak
thesecondshelf.com

21

OWL BOOKSHOP

North London's literary nest

Beloved by Kentish Towners who don't seem to mind that it's been quietly bought out by indie chain Daunt, Owl is still a thriving autonomous bookshop catering to the interests of its regulars. Alongside a dizzying amount of new and classic fiction, there are big sections on travel – with an impressive number of Lonely Planet guides and Ordnance Survey maps for explorers – and large sections covering gardening, sport, cooking, humour, wellness and pregnancy. And for those already sprogged, one whole side of the roomy shop is devoted to children's books for all ages, from young-adult graphic novels and school textbooks to a colourful wall of picture books for teeny ones.

207–209 Kentish Town Road, NW5 2JU
Nearest station: Kentish Town
owlbookshop.co.uk

22

AMNESTY INTERNATIONAL BOOKSHOP

Top-tier charity finds

Want to feel good about adding to your already heaving bookshelves? Take a trip to the Amnesty International bookshop. There are lots of brand-new titles here (thanks to generous donations from locals), but it still retains that anarchic thrill of second-hand discovery, overseen by posters detailing Amnesty's great work. There are rare editions as well as books on travel, nature, cooking (even some recent Ottolenghi titles), philosophy, human rights, feminism, the NHS, self-care and a nice load of literature in other languages. Come for the cause and the books, stay for the jazz, the friendly staff and the shelves of giftable candles, soaps and other trinkets.

308 Kentish Town Road, NW5 2TH
Nearest station: Kentish Town
Other location: Hammersmith
amnesty.org.uk/amnesty-bookshops

23

HOUSMANS BOOKSHOP

A welcoming home for London's left-wingers

Over the course of more than 60 years, Housmans has shared its Cally Road premises with *Peace News*, the Gay Liberation Front, Greenpeace and the CND. The shop's radical heritage is still on full display via its wide range of books and zines on economics, international politics, feminism and labour history (with whole shelves for Chomsky and Orwell). Politics types will drool over archive copies of *Spare Rib*, *Liberation* and *Class War*, and this is also the place to bag slogan badges and postcards. The vibe is warm and welcoming: pay-it-forward vouchers subsidise books for those who wouldn't be able to afford them, and there's a discount for students and union members. Bonus: you can hear tube trains rumbling underneath as you browse.

5 Caledonian Road, N1 9DY
Nearest station: King's Cross St Pancras
housmans.com

24

BOOKBAR

Bookshop by day, bar by night

Enter this friendly bookshop-cafe-bar and you'll be greeted with the smell of fresh coffee. During the day, browse the eye-catching shelves (note the team's 'desert island read' recommendations) before settling down at the central table with an oat flat white and a new release. Downstairs, there are a few more tables where laptops are allowed, as well as a blackboard wall of customer recommendations for anyone feeling indecisive. Once night falls, the wine and negronis start flowing. It's open until 9pm from Wednesday to Saturday, so stop by for one of the regular events or to enjoy a solo date with a good book and a good glass of pinot noir.

166 Blackstock Road, N5 1HA
Nearest station: Arsenal
bookbaruk.com

25

WALDEN BOOKS

Pre-loved bliss off the beaten path

Appearing like a mirage in the middle of a row of terraced houses, Walden is a tranquil retreat from the mayhem of Camden Town. It's been here since 1979, and is such an institution that it sells postcards of its own shopfront. Paperbacks crammed onto trolleys outside go for as little as £1 each, while the inside rooms – lined with crowded, skew-whiff shelves – are silent except for creaking floorboards and the ding of the bell announcing another customer. The average age of the books here must be at least 70, brought way up by the antiquarian cabinet of treasures housed in what looks like an old chimney flue.

38 Harmood Street, NW1 8DP
Nearest station: Kentish Town West
waldenbooks.co.uk

26

WORD ON THE WATER

London's only floating bookshop

This wonderful bookshop on a boat had been floating up and down London's canals for a few years before finding a permanent mooring in King's Cross. Now it livens up a stretch of the towpath near Coal Drops Yard with a blasting jazz playlist and (in summer) boxes of second-hand books for open-air browsing, not to mention the deck-top stage for occasional live gigs and readings. Step inside (mind your head – seriously) and you're immersed in a wooden cocoon decked out with colourful shelves. Tapestry rugs, squishy armchairs and cushion-strewn nooks dial up the cosiness. Just don't let the gentle rocking of the barge lull you to sleep.

Regent's Canal Towpath, N1C 4LW
Nearest station: King's Cross St Pancras
wordonthewater.co.uk

27
PRIMROSE HILL BOOKS

Combine celeb-spotting and book buying

With literary legends including Ted Hughes, Sylvia Plath, Keats *and* Yeats once living locally, it makes sense that Primrose Hill has a suitably prestigious bookseller. In a neighbourhood that can feel a bit chi-chi, this long-standing literary establishment (family-run for over 35 years) is nothing but warm and authentic, well-loved and delightfully well-worn. Outside are crates of second-hand goodies. Inside, new books are slotted into every available space: stacked high on tables, piled in towers on the faded carpet, balanced on wonky carousels. Be sure to look out for the big selection of signed copies by illustrious locals (and try to stay cool if you spot any of Primrose Hill's celebrity residents popping in for a browse).

134 Regent's Park Road, NW1 8XL
Nearest station: Chalk Farm
primrosehillbooks.com

28

BOOM CAT BOOKS

Covert Camden Market spot

Formerly Black Gull, this hole-in-the-wall bookshop in Camden's Lock Market has been taken over (by a former employee) and renamed, but remains a bibliophile need-to-know. Surprisingly quiet considering the hustle and bustle around the food stalls outside, its mostly-second-hand stock includes an unusually wide selection of fantasy, sci-fi and horror fiction, plus books on religious and occult matters – along with more down-to-earth paperbacks. A few new books outside retail at £7 a pop, and there's also an assorted box of second-hand vinyl. As befits the Camden location, the atmosphere is pleasingly countercultural: Extinction Rebellion and Class War stickers in the window, and a sign advertising a free Amazon Alexa with every copy of *Nineteen Eighty-Four.*

70-71 West Yard, Camden Lock Place, London, NW1 8AF
Nearest station: Camden Town
camdenmarket.com/shops/boom-cat-books

29

INK@84 BOOKS

A paper palooza

It's clear that the people who run this fiercely independent local bookshop love print, ink and paper. Not only is there a wealth of carefully selected fiction (plus a small non-fiction section), but you'll also find exquisite Cambridge Imprint patterned notebooks, illustrated cards, framed art prints, beautiful hand-printed animal garlands and colourful wrapping paper. At the back, there's a lovely kids' section with a dangerously cute wall of toys and games. They also sell candles, hot water bottles and silly bookmarks – all the ingredients for the ultimate cosy reading session.

84 Highbury Park, N5 2XE
Nearest station: Arsenal
ink84bookshop.co.uk

30

NEW BEACON BOOKS

Venerable Black bookshop and publishing house

Founded in 1966 by activist and poet John La Rose and his partner Sarah White as England's first Caribbean publishing house, New Beacon was a footloose bookshop (including a spell operating from various living rooms) before settling in Finsbury Park. In its present-day form it is a hub of Black British history and culture, with shelves containing radical pamphlets, zines and hefty political paperbacks; volumes on every topic relating to the African diaspora, from Black cinema to Caribbean cookery; plus dedicated sections for Central and South America, Asia and the Middle East. Saved by crowdfunding twice in recent years, its community value is undeniable – and with reggae on the stereo and a well-used noticeboard in the hallway, it's as welcoming a place as you'd hope for.

76 Stroud Green Road, N4 3EN
Nearest station: Finsbury Park
newbeaconbooks.com

31

PICKLED PEPPER BOOKS

Where tiny bookworms reign supreme

Crouch End is a parental paradise, home to a glorious toy shop and kids' hairdresser, as well as this ace bookshop for small people. The shelves are lined with titles for all ages from *That's Not My Kitten* through to *The Hunger Games* – but it's especially good for the under-fives crowd, with daily play and creative sessions, picture-book author signings and even a theatre in the back room for babies and toddlers. Staff will help you tailor your purchases to your little ones' latest phases, whether you want books about nature and science, history or dance – or put your trust in the in-house 'book fairies' to deliver a customised subscription or one-off bundle.

10 Middle Lane, N8 8PL
Nearest station: Hornsey
pickledpepperbooks.co.uk

32

STOKE NEWINGTON BOOKSHOP

Family-friendly Stokey stalwart

As an area boasting its own annual literary festival, it's no surprise that Stoke Newington's indie bookshop is one of the city's greats. Since 1987, Hackney readers young and old have flocked here for wordy nourishment. There's a lot packed into the iconic blue shelves and tables, from cookery to crime, graphic novels to gardening and a strong range of new fiction. Don't be put off by the abnormally high concentration of smug post-brunch couples impressing each other with how well-read they are; the vibe here is very relaxed, especially for families. There's a particularly extensive children's section, home to an enormous cuddly teddy, plus another toy and bookshop a few doors down dedicated to small readers.

159 Stoke Newington High St, N16 0NY
Nearest station: Stoke Newington
stokenewingtonbookshop.co.uk

33

LIBRERIA

Hip hub that treads its own path

Run by Second Home (the deliciously retro-futuristic workspace across the road), Libreria is determined to do things differently. Its lamp-lit, canary yellow walls with gigantic mirrors stretching across the back and ceiling create an illusion of infinite, undulating shelves. Books are organised by theme – time and space, brain and being, wanderlust or the city – rather than topic or author, and include pithily written staff recommendations. Don't miss the children's corner tucked away at the back, with mini versions of the reading nooks that dot the main space. And check the events schedule: Libreria's book launches attract all sorts of big thinkers, from philosophers to journalists and scientists – there are some fun poetry nights, too.

65 Hanbury Street, E1 5JP
Nearest station: Shoreditch High Street
libreria.io

34

DONLON BOOKS

Hackney's most Hackney bookshop

There's a reason that Donlon is the favourite London shop of John Waters, cult film director and 'Pope of Trash'. This is a hyper-eclectic cabinet of curiosities curated by the man behind the counter: Irish fashion graduate Conor Donlon. On any given visit you might find fanzines, photo pamphlets on Northern Soul and 1980s punk, self-published art monographs, vintage pornography, rare Japanese editions in the antiquarian cabinet and the latest non-fiction releases covering queer heroes, psyche-delics, counterculture, tarot cards and plant magic. There are no signposted sections, which makes browsing amid the bold, Bauhaus-coloured walls a voyage of discovery. Too cool for school? Maybe, but there's no other London bookshop like it.

75 Broadway Market, e8 4ph
Nearest station: London Fields
donlonbooks.com

35

BURLEY FISHER BOOKS

Quintessential neighbourhood indie

Hackney is blessed with several lovely independent bookshops, but Burley Fisher is up there with the best. It opened in a high-ceilinged former hair salon in 2016, helmed by writer Samuel Fisher and bookseller Jason Burley, and has been the London finalist for Independent Bookshop of the Year an astonishing four times. Its strengths include impeccable staff recommendations (both bespoke and via its blog and podcast), a busy calendar of literary events, including an annual eponymous festival, and a cute cafe with tables at the back. It's a shop, a hangout and a hub of bookish culture in the area.

400 Kingsland Road, E8 4AA
Nearest station: Haggerston
burleyfisherbooks.com

36

THE BROADWAY BOOKSHOP

An independent that means business

A few steps before the frivolity of Broadway Market really kicks off, this is a thoughtful literary bookshop staffed by passionate book people. The front section hosts new titles, poetry and writing on music and art, while the larger mezzanine room, down a narrow, well-worn staircase, is packed with travel, philosophy and essays. Below that lies a small but well-stocked kids and YA section. There's an almost intimidating breadth and depth for a modest shop (with the hefty stock complimented by special displays of second-hand French books, a whole shelf of blue-and-white Fitzcarraldo Editions and a handful of upmarket cards and notebooks). For casual browsers, there's always something interesting on the counter display.

6 Broadway Market, E8 4QJ
Nearest station: Cambridge Heath
broadwaybookshophackney.com

37

KOENIG BOOKS

Achingly chic art books

Founded in Cologne in the 1960s, publishers and booksellers Koenig now operate a fleet of shops in Europe's most illustrious galleries and museums. Its two current London outposts are at the Serpentine and Whitechapel Galleries; both sites are elegant, serious-minded and supremely well-stocked. Art is king here, naturally: the range of artists represented, from Old Masters to experimental newcomers, is hard to beat. But as well as the full range of visual culture (including its self-published titles), Koenig dishes up the freshest and most incisive literature, criticism and magazines as carefully as any gallery – displaying many books cover-out as works of art in themselves.

Whitechapel High Street, E1 7QX
Nearest station: Aldgate East
Other location: Kensington
buchhandlung-walther-koenig.de

38

FREEDOM PRESS

Whitechapel's anarchist haven

Considering that it's been trading from roughly the same address since 1942, it's surprisingly tricky finding Britain's oldest and largest anarchist bookshop. And it's no wonder, given that the shop and press have survived firebombing, fascist attacks, redevelopment and state repression. But duck down dingy Angel Alley, enter through the doorway on your left and you'll be surrounded by revolutionary literature: politics, society, history, environment, liberation movements, art and culture, and some added fiction with a political or utopian bent (particularly sci-fi). Leaflets, pamphlets, zines, postcards, prints and memorabilia are here too, bolstering Freedom's lineage as an anarchist publisher dating back to 1886. Long may they continue advocating for a fairer world.

84b Whitechapel High Street, E1 7QX
Nearest station: Aldgate East
freedompress.org.uk

39

BRICK LANE BOOKSHOP

A London-loving independent

The long-serving, community-focused Brick Lane Bookshop is the only booksellers on this famous London street – a responsibility it takes seriously. It's one big, welcoming, open-plan room with section titles chalked above the shelves. Areas of focus include music books, kids' books, poetry and fiction, and the shop runs an annual short story competition and publishes the winners. The real selling point, though, is right at the front of the shop, in what must be the capital's most enlightening display of London's past and present through guides, maps, fiction and journalism. If you want to learn more about the city, especially the East End, this is the best place to start.

166 Brick Lane, E1 6RU
Nearest station: Shoreditch High Street
bricklanebookshop.org

40

ARTWORDS BOOKSHOP

Visually-led books and magazines

This good-looking Hackney spot, a stone's throw from the Hoxton Mini Press office, is a design-lover's paradise. Most books here are displayed cover-out and careful attention is given to the rotating colour-coordinated window displays. Alongside a plethora of fashion, art and photography books – plus plenty of cookbooks and how-tos for home and garden – Artwords is a go-to for zeitgeisty magazines. Get your *Cabana*, your *Noble Rot*, your *Popeye* and your *Numéro* here (and ask at the desk for back issues). There's also an impeccable choice of small-format paperbacks, including philosophy, spirituality, society, memoir and the hottest fiction, plus perhaps London's most stylish kids' section.

20–22 Broadway Market, E8 4QJ
Nearest station: London Fields
Other location: Hackney Central
artwords.co.uk

41

THE COMMON PRESS BOOKSHOP

Big-hearted queer hangout

It doesn't get any more inclusive than this welcoming bookshop-cafe at the top of Brick Lane. Identifying as London's first consciously queer intersectional bookshop, they sell a comprehensive selection of LGBTQIA+ authors and radical books on Black history, disability studies, environmentalism, consumerism, fourth-wave feminism and poetry, graphic novels and horror (including stories of gay werewolves). The wonderfully diverse children's books explore migration, self, community and gender. And there's a lot more going on here than reading and coffee: Common Press hosts dance, yoga and book clubs by day and night.

118 Bethnal Green Road, E2 6DG
Nearest station: Shoreditch High Street
commonpress.co.uk

42

LONDON CENTRE FOR BOOK ARTS

The nuts and bolts of bookmaking

What goes into physically making a book from scratch? If you head to the LCBA, they'll show you. There are tonnes of beginner's courses in book-binding, letterpress printing and publishing at their colourful Hackney Wick bookshop and studio, with a well-equipped workspace for more experienced makers. The bookshop itself is a treat for anyone who likes beautifully made books. Chances are, you won't recognise any of the titles here: there's a wide-ranging selection including books on alternative subcultures, craft, design, papermaking, typography, printmaking, creative communities and, of course, bookmaking – plus all the tools if you're inspired to give it a go back at home.

Britannia Works, 56 Dace Road, E3 2NQ
Nearest station: Hackney Wick
londonbookarts.org

43

PAGES OF HACKNEY

Beloved Hackney community hub

The good vibes are tangible in Clapton's only bookshop with its Pay It Forward solidarity board displayed prominently by the till. This is a true community bookshop with a holistic selection that feels like a little microcosm of its diverse Hackney enclave. There are shelves dedicated to politics, architecture, urbanism, cycling, cookery, gardening and parenting, as well as sections emphasising Black British writing, gender, sexuality, feminism and Afrofuturism. There's even a lovely curation of children's books on self, identity and wellbeing, as well as a wall of second-hand finds. Grab a seat on the comfy yellow velvet sofa downstairs and dive into a political essay or a vintage poetry book.

70 Lower Clapton Road, E5 0RN
Nearest station: Hackney Central
pagesofhackney.co.uk

44

THE BOOKSHOP
ON THE HEATH

Picture-perfect home of rare books

The name says it all: this handsome second-hand bookshop overlooks the rolling turf and fancy houses of Blackheath, making the most of its enviable position with a hard-to-miss teal and gold paint job. The atmosphere inside is genteel and charming: blue carpet, slightly ramshackle varnished wooden shelves and three rooms of leatherbound volumes, Folio Society editions and £2 paperbacks, plus posters and prints with a focus on local history. Pick up a smart (yet affordable) read and head to the wine bar next door to live your best bookworm life over a glass of red.

74 Tranquil Vale, SE3 0BW
Nearest station: Blackheath
bookshopontheheath.co.uk

45

MOROCCO BOUND

Books, beans, beers and beyond

The name of this friendly bookshop-bar-cafe-events space-cultural centre ('embrace the ambiguity, man' says their website) is a play on its address and the area's history of leather tanning. But you won't find any hidebound tomes here – just a lovingly curated selection of contemporary writing and fanzines on offer with locally brewed lagers and pale ales. As well as championing local authors and breweries, this is a relaxed community hub; the shelves are sprinkled with hand-scribbled recommendations and the walls adorned with photos of staff and regulars. With unusually late opening hours, nights here include book clubs, poetry open mics and writing workshops, plus gigs, comedy and quizzes. All a great opportunity to sample the excellent prose and pints.

1a Morocco Street, SE1 3HB
Nearest station: London Bridge
moroccobound.co.uk

46

MARCUS CAMPBELL ART BOOKS

Arty second-hand boutique

Over the road from Tate Modern, this glass-fronted spot may not look as impressive as its Brutalist neighbour but it's packed with just as many artistic big-hitters (and you can even take some home with you). Trading from here for 25 years, Marcus Campbell specialises in rare and out-of-print (read: expensive) art publications, hence the studious vibe. A vitrine displays antiquarian gems for hundreds or thousands, and the shelves are packed with massive hardback monographs. But for more casual art-lovers, there are new and remaindered books, pamphlets and cheaper monographs on a central table, and lucky-dip bargain bins from £1 to £5 full of intriguing titles. Missed an exhibition recently? You might just find the catalogue here.

43 Holland St, SE1 9JR
Nearest station: Blackfriars
marcuscampbell.co.uk

47

SOUTH LONDON GALLERY BOOKSHOP

Eclectic mix for culture vultures

This isn't your standard collection of art books. Alongside the media, performance, photography, architecture, design and art-theory shelves you'd expect, there's a genuinely varied range of experimental fiction and books on race, gender, politics and the environment. Look out for illustrated guides to mushrooms, musings on bad taste, kids' books on pronouns and whimsical photo essays of cats in windows. If it *is* serious art you want, they also publish their own excellent exhibition books and sell reasonably priced artist editions, from prints to pottery. Once you've had your fill of culture, drop into the gallery's cafe, South London Louie, for a hearty cheese toastie.

65 Peckham Road, SE5 8UH
Nearest station: Peckham Rye
shop.southlondongallery.org

48

TERRACE SHOP, TATE MODERN

Extensive visual emporium

London's powerhouse of 20th century art doesn't have just one decent bookshop; it has three. But the Terrace Shop in the relatively new Blavatnik Building has the widest selection, with a long wall of large-format, illustrated titles dedicated to all things visual. Photography, drawing, ceramics, collage, fashion, architecture, design... take your pick. Amid the coffee-table tomes, you'll find art history and theory books, artist biographies and approachable guides to help you launch your own Tate-worthy career. There's an excellent selection of magazines (*Artforum*, *ArtReview*, *Frieze*, et cetera) plus a great children's section, with DIY activity books to turn your kid into a budding Yayoi Kusama.

Bankside, SE1 9TG
Nearest station: Blackfriars
shop.tate.org.uk

49

NATIONAL THEATRE BOOKSHOP

Mighty repository of stagecraft

The NT's unassuming yet extensive range of theatre books performs an indispensable service to London's playgoers, thesps and directors. Tucked away behind a colourful gift shop, there's a whole wall of plays, ordered from Aeschylus to Ziegler. There are scripts for everything on in the West End, plus staff recommendations and areas showcasing Black and Asian playwrights and disabled and LGBTQIA+ narratives. Manuals on every aspect of stagecraft instruct on writing and directing as well as puppetry and stage combat. One shelf has every Shakespeare play in multiple editions, while another is packed with monologues, ready for your next audition. And it all helps fund the theatre's artistic work.

National Theatre, Upper Ground, SE1 9PX
Nearest station: Waterloo
shop.nationaltheatre.org.uk

50

RYE BOOKS

New releases, flat whites and George the dog

The first thing you'll notice when entering this East Dulwich bookshop-cafe is George, the shaggy shop dog splayed in front of the counter. Four-legged friends are more than welcome here – in fact, they're positively encouraged. Each year, the book-shop produces a calendar of canine customers, whose owners come to browse and end up staying for a coffee and a chat. There's no signage on the minimal plywood bookshelves, so you can drift freely from plants to politics and everything in between. Locals pop in to pick up pre-ordered books on everything from children's poetry to The Chemical Brothers, and there are little reading nooks built into the ply bookshelves for kids (or dogs) to get cosy.

47 North Cross Road, SE22 9ET
Nearest station: East Dulwich
ryebooks.co.uk

51

GARDEN MUSEUM SHOP

Make some new fronds

Whether you're a green-fingered guru or wanted for houseplant homicide, the Garden Museum will inspire you to get your hands dirty. Dramatically set in an ancient, deconsecrated church on the river, the museum recounts the histories of the greatest gardens and gardeners, looking at why and how we grow things – and their small bookshop does the same. There are books on guerrilla gardening and formal flower arranging, plant folklore and forests, as well as lush photography books spotlighting famous British gardens from Sissinghurst Castle to Derek Jarman's bleak but breathtaking Dungeness outpost. Look out for the cookbook from the museum's unusually excellent restaurant.

Lambeth Palace Road, SE1 7LB
Nearest station: Vauxhall
gardenmuseum.org.uk

52

BOOKMONGERS

Big bargains in Brixton

A friendly warren of second-hand and remaindered books, Bookmongers has been a Coldharbour Lane institution for 30 years. This higgledy-piggledy cavern has been sectioned off into mini-rooms crammed with different topics: Marxism, socialism and anarchism; occult and spirituality; fiction grouped by author nationality and gender; recent bestsellers; Greek and Roman classics; copious sci-fi novels; and a slew of rock biographies to match the 1970s tunes playing on the shop stereo. At the back you'll find a cosy mezzanine and a big squashy sofa for readers. Mind the cat bowls: they belong to resident feline Popeye (hence the sign for 'No Dogs'), successor to long-serving, much-missed canine staff Leo and Rosa.

439 Coldharbour Lane, SW9 8LN
Nearest station: Brixton
bookmongers.com

53

ROUND TABLE BOOKS

Inclusive and community-led shop

At the centre of buzzing Brixton Market, Round Table started as a crowd-funded inclusive children's bookshop. Now catering to grown-ups too, co-directors Aimée and Meera put global-majority, queer and disabled authors centre-stage with a selection that spans poetry to cookbooks and forward-thinking kids' stories. Alongside its brilliantly diverse selection of books from under-represented writers, Round Table donate books for families, schools and food banks, and partner with Brixton Library and St Thomas' Hospital. With only enough space for a few visitors at a time, the dedicated team have read most of what they've got in stock and are eager to offer personal recommendations to help you navigate the packed shelves.

73 Granville Arcade, Coldharbour Lane, SW9 8PS
Nearest station: Brixton
roundtablebooks.co.uk

54

SOUTH BANK BOOK MARKET

An alfresco institution, open daily

For 40 years, booksellers have laid out their wares on trestle tables by the Thames. The South Bank Book Market isn't as extensive or historic as the Parisian *bouquiniste* stalls that inspired it, but sheltered by an arch of Waterloo Bridge, it's well suited to British weather. The number of stalls peaks at eight each weekend when this stretch of embankment bustles with tourists, day-tripping families and solo browsers. Political memoirs sit alongside graphic novels, Solzhenitsyn and Jackie Collins, travel guides and Harry Potter, in conditions ranging from mint to moderately worn. This may not be the finest (or best-priced) selection in town, but the cosmopolitan experience of browsing by the riverside makes a visit essential.

Queen's Walk, SE1 8TX
Nearest station: Waterloo
southbankcentre.co.uk/visit/shopping/
south-bank-book-market

55

HURLINGHAM BOOKS

An unruly Aladdin's cave

Not one for claustrophobes, this Thames-side treasure trove is legendary for its towering stacks of literature. Second-hand books fill the windows, cascade from floor to ceiling and spill from ramshackle shelves. It's not a big place, but there's more crammed in here than you'd find in shops three times its size. From the chaos emerge brief flashes of order – a run of Shakespeares here, snatches of alphabetisation there – but mostly, Hurlingham is book soup. (And Ray, the owner since 1968, says he has a warehouse nearby with more than a million more.) Surrender to serendipity and pick out whatever catches your eye: it's all well priced, if just a little overwhelming.

91 Fulham High Street, sw6 3js
Nearest station: Putney Bridge
hurlinghambooks.com

56

JOHN SANDOE BOOKS

Chelsea's most charming bookshop

Tucked away just off the King's Road since 1957, Sandoe's stocks (innumerable) new books but has the ramshackle excitement of a second-hand gold mine. Its roots lie in those long-forgotten days when Chelsea was London's most bohemian district, and the shop has stayed true to this welcoming, eclectic spirit despite the tides of oligarch wealth now sloshing around. Tread its well-worn rugs and floorboards and you'll detect an inclination towards history, politics and the arts, as well as the classics. There's usually just one of each title on display, stacked ingeniously to maximise limited space. And the staff are as clued-up and helpful as you could hope for: make the most of their knowledge with a tailored subscription, each delivery guaranteed to be unique to you.

10 Blacklands Terrace, SW3 2SR
Nearest station: Sloane Square
johnsandoe.com

57
BOOKS FOR COOKS

Gastronomic page-turning paradise

At this Notting Hill stalwart – tables stacked with inspiration and shelves peppered with ceramic fruit, veg, kitsch chef animals and crockery – you may feel as if you've wandered into an eccentric friend's kitchen. Books for Cooks does exactly what it says on the tin, attracting hungry readers with its cookbooks-only curation. From Nigella to Yotam, Delia to Madhur, you'll find all the big names at this recipe refuge – plus plenty you've never heard of. Whether it's German baking, intricate dumpling-making, vegan hotpots or a whole book just on peanut butter, it's all here. The little kitchen out the back even rustles up dishes from a different book each lunchtime. Come early to get a table among the shelves.

4 Blenheim Crescent, W11 1NN
Nearest station: Ladbroke Grove
booksforcooks.com

58

SOKOL BOOKS

Seriously ancient tomes

An eccentric Chelsea landmark with its clock and red paint job, Sokol specialises in the rarest and earliest printed books: anything pre-1650. Some of their inventory was produced only a few decades after the printing press was invented, and Sokol occasionally deals in even older manuscripts. It's quite an experience perusing the weighty leather-bound spines and, with its staircases, mezzanines and views of a hidden cemetery, the three-tiered shop feels like a medieval sage's tower... a spell broken only by the double-deckers whooshing past outside.

239a Fulham Road, SW3 6HY
Nearest station: South Kensington
sokol.co.uk

storia
nati

ophetie
achimi

Le Loyer
livre des Spectres
et visions d'Esp

THE COUNTER SCUFFLE. 1637

E.II
115

59

FOSTER BOOKS

Atmospheric second-hand bounty

Hiding behind a Ladbrokes, this charming time warp of a bookshop has been selling rare and out-of-print publications for over 50 years. Outside the striking bottle-green 18th century shopfront are tables of second-hand wonders for as little as £2. Inside, you'll find an old curiosity shop filled floor to ceiling with first editions, antiquarian allsorts and general miscellanea from which readers can unearth stern instructions on 1950s etiquette or dusty, jacketed collections of Christina Rossetti poems. It can be hard to spot the staff behind the chaotic, overstuffed shelves of crumbling leather-bound books, but there is a method here – everything is catalogued so don't be afraid to ask for something specific, no matter how obscure it may seem.

183 Chiswick High Road, W4 2DR
Nearest station: Turnham Green
fosterbooks.co.uk

60

THE L&R BOOKSHOP

A bibliophile's best friend

'Books and Other Necessities' is the tagline for this light-filled homage to the written word. It was first opened in 2009 by literary agency Lutyens & Rubinstein, and although powerhouse Daunt Books have recently taken over, the wide selection of fiction, non-fiction, poetry, art and children's books still feels handpicked. The mezzanine level is home to eye-catching coffee table books and colourful poetry compilations, while the down-stairs children's selection doubles up as an event space for book launches. There's no end of good gift options here, but splash out on a year-long book subscription for someone special – personalised using a taste-based questionnaire.

21 Kensington Park Road, W11 2EU
Nearest station: Ladbroke Grove
landrbookshop.co.uk

61

THE NOTTING HILL BOOKSHOP

Fictional film bookshop come to life

You may already be familiar with this literary treasure trove if you've seen the classic rom-com. The story goes that Notting Hill local Richard Curtis used to browse here, and the bright blue exterior and extensive travel section inspired the film's fictional bookshop. The store on screen is actually a film set as it wasn't possible to shoot inside the real Notting Hill Bookshop – but this doesn't stop hordes of tourists and Hugh Grant/ Julia Roberts fans from taking selfies outside. Either way, this place is worth a visit. Peruse the famous travel section, an excellent assortment of kids' titles and hampers full of pre-wrapped surprise 'blind date' books – in case you feel like having your own unexpected love affair.

13 Blenheim Crescent, London WII 2EE
Nearest station: Ladbroke Grove
thenottinghillbookshop.co.uk

62

NOMAD BOOKS

Family-friendly Fulham favourite

Nomad was named London's Independent Book-shop of the Year in 2023 – but this corner spot has been treasured by its well-heeled Parsons Green neighbours since opening in 1990. The dark wooden floor of the front room offsets a thoughtful showcase of the latest and greatest titles, but it's Nomad's back section that comprises their secret weapon. A brilliantly bright and inviting kids' room serves up books for babies through to teenagers, excellent gift recommendations and a comfortable sofa where little ones can immerse themselves in print. More to love: the magnificent selection of cards and wrapping paper; the clued-up, helpful booksellers; and the dedicated Francophone sections for the *jeunes* and *moins jeunes*.

781 Fulham Road, SW6 5HA
Nearest station: Parsons Green
nomadbooks.co.uk

63

THE ALLIGATOR'S MOUTH

A children's literature bonanza

The kids of Richmond really are spoiled: not only do they have London's biggest park on their doorstep, but also a delightful children's bookshop. Located down a small path off the high street, it's hard to miss the massive window display of illustrated characters. This place is chock-full of children's books, with a particular soft spot for illustrated editions of classics like *The Wind in the Willows* – and even Darwin's *Origin of Species*. Folk tales and legends also get their own tempting shelf. Check out where various visiting illustrators have left their mark – yep, that's a hand-drawn Gruffalo.

2a Church Court, TW9 1JL
Nearest station: Richmond
thealligatorsmouth.co.uk

64

TASCHEN STORE LONDON

Books big enough to break your shelves

'I just need a bigger home, stronger bookshelves and a pay rise' – a common lament after visiting the Chelsea flagship of luxury publisher TASCHEN. This is true coffee-table book heaven: whether you're into tattoos, seaweed or citrus fruit, there's guaranteed to be a colossal hardback dedicated to it. The kitsch doesn't end with the books, either – with its gold shelving and a rainbow staircase designed by Philippe Starck, even the shop is OTT. And if you think the big books on the ground floor are impressive, the basement gallery downstairs will blow your mind: exquisite limited-edition tomes so gigantic, they require their own bespoke stands and bank loans.

12 Duke of York Square, SW3 4LY
Nearest station: Sloane Square
taschen.com

CONTRIBUTORS

Sonya Barber and James Manning started working together professionally in 2012 and romantically in 2016. Sonya has written three other books in this series for Hoxton Mini Press and contributed to publications including *Condé Nast Traveller*; James is an editor at *Time Out*. They live together in east London with their daughter and cat.

Hoxton Mini Press is a small indie publisher based in east London. We make books about London (and beyond) with a dedication to lovely, sustainable production and brilliant photography. When we started the company, people told us 'print was dead'; we wanted to prove them wrong. Books are no longer just about information but objects in their own right: things to collect and own and inspire. We are an environmentally conscious publisher, committed to offsetting our carbon footprint. This book, for instance, is 100 per cent carbon compensated, with offset purchased from Stand for Trees.

*An Opinionated Guide
to London Bookshops*
First edition. Second printing.

Published in 2024 by Hoxton Mini Press,
London. Copyright © Hoxton Mini Press
2024. All rights reserved.

Text by Sonya Barber and James Manning.
Editing by Zoë Jellicoe. Proofreading by
Florence Ward. Design and production by
Richard Mason. Editorial support by Leona
Crawford. With thanks to Matthew Young
for initial series design.

Please note: we recommend checking the
websites listed for each entry before you
visit for the latest information on price,
opening times and pre-booking
requirements.

ISBN: 978-1-914314-66-7

Printed and bound by OZGraf, Poland

Hoxton Mini Press is an environmentally
conscious publisher, committed to offsetting
our carbon footprint. This book is 100 per
cent carbon compensated, with offset
purchased from Stand For Trees.

Every time you order from our website,
we plant a tree: www.hoxtonminipress.com

Selected opinionated guides in the series:

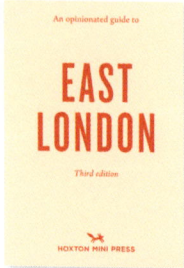

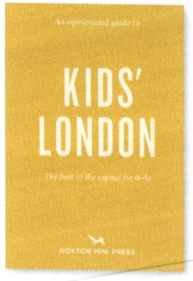

For more go to *www.hoxtonminipress.com*

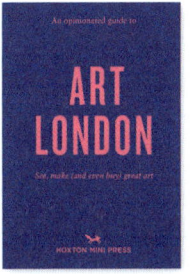

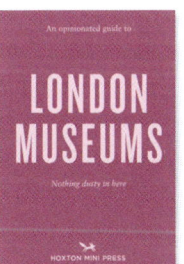

INDEX